KISS FROM GOD

KISS FROM GOD

Stephanie Sorady

Copyright © 2021 by Stephanie Sorady

All rights reserved. no part of this publication may be reproduced, distributed ut the prior written permission of the publisher, except in the case of brief quotations embodied in critical reviews and certain other noncommercial uses permitted by copyright law. For permission requests, write to the publisher, addressed "attention: Permissions Coordinator," at the e-mail address below.

davina@alegriamagazine.com

Library of Congress Control number: 2021917161

ISBN: 978-1-7361496-7-6

Published by alegria Publishing
Book cover and layout by Carlos Mendoza

To all the souls who've ever feared they were broken, may this book be a reminder that your uniqueness is a Kiss From God.

"She stood there until something fell off the shelf inside her. Then she went inside there to see what it was."

Zora Neale Hurston, *Their Eyes Were Watching God*

Preface

I wrote my first poem as a homework assignment in the third grade. The assignment was to write a poem about a place we love. I wrote about my abuelita (grandma's) house in Acapulco Mexico. Although I was only about eight years old, poetry provided me the space to explore feelings of longing, love, and what it was like growing up in two cultures. Once I finished my poem (aptly titled "My Acapulco Home") I decided to share it with my beautiful, hard-working, immigrant mother. With excitement and nerves running through my body, I handed her my scribbled piece of paper. She read it intently for a long while before, finally, a smile appeared on her face, and she said, "Mija esto es arte." *my daughter, this is art.* That bit of encouragement was all it took. I was hooked. Reading and writing became my greatest companions in life.

While writing this book, I kept that younger version of myself front of mind to help motivate and inspire my work. I also thought about other past versions of me that struggled with loss, anxiety, depression, addictive behaviors and chronically feeling like I was never "enough" for this world. Versions of me that wanted so desperately to feel seen and believe that healing was possible. Then, I imagined other young women who might be feeling that same aching loneliness. I wrote this book for younger me, for you, for us.

My hope in sharing these poems with you is that you may experience some bit of the comfort and hope that books and poetry have long given me. I may not know you, but I know if you're reading this right now you've likely struggled with similar issues that I have. At times, you've quietly (or loudly) worried that you were "broken" and simply not "enough" for this big, loud, and scary world. This collection of poems is meant to be a reminder that you are far from broken. You are more than enough exactly as you are. If you get nothing else from reading my writing, I truly hope you take that truth with you.

A Bit About the Title and Cover

The title of this collection *Kiss From God* comes from not one but *two* poems in this book, which I can't wait for you to read. The phrase is inspired by a unique purple birthmark covering my left arm. The birthmark has faded a lot throughout my life, but it's a combination of purple splotches that swirl and twist around my hand and arm. As a little girl, my mom and dad were worried that people would make strange comments, ask awkward questions, and make me feel "weird." To combat any feelings of shame I might develop around my birthmark, they made a vow to never cover it up or try to downplay it. So when other kids and plenty of adults inevitably asked, "What's that on your arm?" little toddler Stephanie began to confidently answer, "This is a Kiss From God!" The cover art of this book is a flower inspired by that very birthmark: bright, purple, vibrant and eager to be seen. May these poems serve as reminders that the things that make you different, the things that make you wonder if you're "weird," are actually proof that *you* are a Kiss From God.

<u>Who Likes Poetry?</u>

Observers,
        Listeners,
Dreamers,
        Thinkers.

The type of person who pulls
meaning out of the mundane,
or hears the song within a name.

The type of person who wonders
what the color turquoise might taste like.

The type of person who sees,
the connection between all things.

You know who likes poetry?
        Poets do.

Tiny Prayer

Make me smaller
I beg the Lord.
Ten years old,
carrying the weight of knowing
that this body will only
continue to grow.

I can no longer take
suggestions from the women
I know the perfect diet for you,
eat only apples for the next three days...

Creeping gazes from the men
as they proclaim
My how you've grown,
If only I were your age...

Either way I am left
with the impression
that I've somehow sinned.

Tiny hands press together
like a fleshy pink steeple,
Make me smaller - please!
A devoted hunger in my tone

A good girl is all I want to be.

Stephanie Sorady

Panic Attack

Lying in bed
with the man I love,
all I seek is pleasure
and then welcome rest.

But even here you find me,
my cruel companion.

First you press hard and rough
into my soft bare chest.
Next you seize me by the palms,
slick, hot, and wet.

Always one to do your best,
I'm aware that next
you'll paw your way
down beneath my breasts,
to claim my pounding heart.

Insatiable as you are
and never afraid to go too far,
you finish it all by taking my mind,
leaving it aching, pained and paralyzed.

I am neither alive nor dead
as you slink out of bed
Your lust momentarily quenched.

I feel a heat rise
in the back of my neck,
While your voice echoes in my head,

Until next time.

For Kids That Grew Up Fast

Some kids don't get to stay kids for long,
some kids are the peacemakers,
some kids are the comforters,
some kids are the caretakers,
some kids are the babysitters

Even when those kids
are grown and on their own
they still need to know:
It's okay to want
to need, to hurt
to bleed, to feel joy
to say no. It is even okay
to let them go.

Stephanie Sorady

Hurt People

Can you hear the depths of his pain?
In the way he howls at anyone who dares
to believe he is worthy of good things.

Can you feel the enormity of her grief?
How it burned her heart and soul
leaving behind twisted scars and little room for hope?

Can you taste the bitterness of their isolation?
Salty, sharp and harsh. To be told and over and over again
"there is no place for you here,"
it's no wonder they would rather hide.

Do you know what it's like to feel
unloved, unwanted, and abandoned?
Of course you do. Everyone does.

> Remember that the next time
> you see another human
> arming themselves for protection,
> hiding in their isolation,
> or lashing out with cold
> and cut-throat words.
> Because in reality the only thing
> they actually want someone
> to hear is *help*.

When She Drinks

Her eyes get glossy,
        my gut gets tight.

Her temper grows shorter,
       my armor grows
tougher.

Her glass is empty,
        and so is my hope.

Stephanie Sorady

Depression

Creeps and creaks
in the back of my mind
until the creeping & creaking
becomes clanking & clunking
then the clanking & clunking
turns into crying & calling
for help.

Except no one else,
can hear a sound.

Toxic Part

The part of me that can't stop,
thinking about you,
is a small, but active,
portion of my brain.

I imagine the neurons clustered there
are constantly writhing
in pleasure or pain.

The part of me that can't stop,
wanting you,
is probably the same part of me
that doesn't know when
enough is enough.

The part that likes to
drink all night
lay in bed all day.

The part that says it's okay,
to eat tubs of ice cream
or nothing at all.

The part that curses your name,
then answers your calls.

The part of me that can't stop,
loving you,
is the same part,

That doesn't believe
I deserve any love at all.

Stephanie Sorady

<u>Somedays</u>

Some days, we cannot hear how beautifully the ocean sings
or gaze in awe at the movement of a hummingbird's wings.

Somedays, our pain is too great to make space for tomorrow.
Some days, we need to wrap our hearts in compassion
and cool our burning minds with generous doses of stillness.

Some days, it's okay that things are not okay,
and on these days, we give ourselves the gift of rest,
nothing more, nothing less.

Self-Love Journey

Each step is for my younger sister
and future daughter,
so that they might spend less
time and money digging
the needs of others out
from beneath their fingernails.

Each small win is taken
in honor of my grandmothers
who redirected their own dreams
to birth the futures of others.

Each time I allow myself
to wield the power of
saying *no*, younger me
is less afraid, less alone.

Do not forget that each
time you take this road,
lined with compassion,
intuition, and love you
give another woman out
there a piece of the map,
so she can do the same.

Stephanie Sorady

Sober

Sober, Sow-burr... Sober?
I toss the word around in my mouth

And attempt to effortlessly roll it off my tongue
with the hummed ease of Spanish r's,

But it's all clunky and messy and it's still too loud in my mind
to speak, or think. Maybe I need a drink?

Sober... I Google everything. Celebrities that abstain,
the damage booze does to your brain

Or worse - the wrinkles it gives your face!
Sob stories, success stories, I wonder,

What do I want to be my story?
Sober... It's a poison, no doubt.

But it feels so good when that first sip
hits my eager mouth.

Sober... Okay but - what if I like the taste?
Of cheap fermented grapes,

Of fitting in, and having a place.
Dumb, numb but not the only one.

Sober... Alright well don't I deserve a break?
Because feeling things all the time,

Is fucking hard. And so what if sometimes
maybe every other time, I take it too far?
Sober... Secrets slipping as I continue sipping my release.
Slowly obliterating all that's mine.

Surely this is the same as peace,
even though I wake up to a crumbling mind,

Sweaty back, and tender heart.
Because if not, then I've been doing this

All wrong... Sober. Sober. Sober.

Stephanie Sorady

To My Addiction
Part 1

I want you to take me
to the far away places,
the upside down spaces,
take me away without a trace,

So that the hard bits of life,
will not find me.
Well, at least not until
the crude signs of morning.

Tug on my strings
until you've unraveled me from within,
because I'm tired of tightening
the rusted hinges of my heart,
meant to keep it all in.

I'll let you have me,
body and soul,
but in return I have one request,
that you tell no one
of the strange places we go.

To My Addiction
Part 2

Unbearable,
unreliable,
undone,
that is who I was
when I was bound to you.

Until one day I realized
It's my tender heart,
that makes me so strong.

Today I'm proud to say,
It's been 365 days
since I last let you
take me away.

Away from my partner,
my friends, and family.
Away from the truth and beauty
that lives inside me.

Unattached from you I am
aligned,
alive,
authentic.

I saved my own life,
and that is something
you will never take from me.

Stephanie Sorady

In Progress

I'm a work in progress.
A portrait of pure love,

the Artist left some flaws in me,
A handful of asymmetries,

But that doesn't mean,
that I am not worthy.

The beauty is the brushstrokes,
the masterpiece is just being.

Addiction Runs in Families

Addiction runs in my family,
and it's been running for a long time.

With effortless speed,
it's torn through
fathers and sons,
mothers and daughters,
brothers and sisters.

Ripping out hearts,
knocking down futures,
leaving no traces of hope behind.

Addiction ran with us,
across oceans
and over borders,
darting in and out of
humble homes
where no one knew
what to do with
all that wreckage.

Addiction ran in my family,
until it ran into me
and I soaked its
feet in cement
and took away its chance
of ever running with us
again.

Stephanie Sorady

Worries

The endless worries
that torment today,
are always far worse
than what actually becomes of
tomorrow.

Negative Thoughts

The next time a gang of negative thoughts
decides to break-in and crash your mind,
I invite you to grab these thoughts and sit them down.

Round up all of the *not enoughs*
the *you're too muchs and* everyone in between,
because it's time to show them who's boss.

Tie them to the chair, shine a bright light
on their cowardly faces then lay all the evidence
right there on the table.

Tell them of the times you fought and won.
Flaunt each penny saved, each love earned.
Confront them with the hard truth:
No matter what life puts you through,
your heart remains soft and your back is strong.

They will make every attempt to scale the walls
and seize your precious heart. But you my friend,
are destined to win,because you have truth
on your side. You're not the type of person
to let such heinous lies live rent free
inside your mind.

The next time those negative thoughts
attempt to stage a coup, remind them
who they are dealing with.

Remind your thoughts,
they answer to you.

Stephanie Sorady

What If...

What if I am not smart enough?
What if I am not strong enough?
What if this life is too much?
What if this life is not enough?
What if they don't love me?
What if I'm not lovable at all?

What if you let go of other people's reactions?
What if you stop trying to control it all?
What if you asked for help?
What if you trust yourself
enough to answer God's call?

<u>Not my Nanny</u>

She is not my nanny,
or my maid.

Yes - we're here together.
No, our skin is not the same.

She is my root,
mi razón de ser.

I will not have
my mother's labors
be in vain.

Stephanie Sorady

Mamá's Morisqueta

My mamá doesn't say *I'm sorry* too often,
especially not when she's in the wrong.
As a kid, I imagined those two tiny words
trapped inside her chest refusing to come out.
As a woman, I imagine how likely it is that no one
ever said them to her when she was young.

My mamá doesn't say *I'm sorry* too often,
but when she does she says it through the gut.
One moment she's shouting that I'm the worst
daughter in the world. That I am ungrateful
That I am the selfish beast she never got to be.

Then suddenly she's serving me a hot plate of morisqueta.
Fluffy white rice piled into my favorite bowl,
drenched in beans, bright red tomato sauce, and
slightly melted cotija cheese beckons for me to eat.
The scent of garlic and onion whisper *I love you,*
and every bite translates to *I will never leave.*

My mamá doesn't say *I'm sorry* too often,
but when I look up from my plate and see her
standing in the kitchen, wiping her hands against
a tattered apron and my belly hums with warmth,
she doesn't need to.

Little Brother

For years I prayed at the ending of each day,
that God would take the loneliness away.
I prayed for comfort, companionship and for
someone who might care about the things
I had to say.

Eleven years, eleven months and ten days
That's how long it took to end the silence
That's how long it took for me to know
what love feels like in your bones,
That's how long it took for me to believe
in miracles,
That's how long it took,
for God to give me you.

Little Sister

I hope that when love calls,
you answer with your lion roar.

I hope that when life
knocks you on your back,
you take time to heal
your wounds a bit before
getting back up for more.

I hope that you never
find yourself speaking
only to discover that
the voice you hear is not your own.

I hope that you become familiar
with your flaws, enough to hold them
in your palms and carry them with compassion.

Little sister, I pray you find God
in whatever form she speaks to you,
and you recognize you're never
actually alone.

Tonight You Died

Tonight
while they sing their hallelujahs
and fill their hearts with hope,
yours was struck with a single shot
by someone who knew you well-enough
to get real close.

Tonight
lo juro por dios
that I felt you leave this world
selfishly taking a piece of me
to the other side.

Tonight
my sink is full of vomit,
my mind is full of nothingness
and your mamacita's screams
linger in the sky above.

Tonight
while your young son sleeps
I do not understand why the world
does not weep for how deeply it failed you.

Stephanie Sorady

Ritual Para Recordar

En una noche como esta,
me siento sofocada por
el olor a casa sola.

Apago las luces,
abro las ventanas,
y me estiro en la cama
que era nuestra.

Rodeada de silencio,
susurros secos y lejanos.

Solo así puedo volver a mirar
tus ojos de mar
y escuchar tu voz,
tierna y lenta.

Solo así llegó a sentir
la calidez de tus brazos
envolviendo mi cintura.

Solo así me atrevo
a ofrecer mi mano
hacia la profunda oscuridad.

Ahí es cuando el viento
y los ancestros
te devuelven a mí.

Y por un momento divino
sé que los muertos
aún viven.

<u>Ritual for Remembering</u>

On a night like tonight,
I feel suffocated by
the smell of an empty home.

I turn off the lights,
open the windows,
and stretch onto the
bed that once was ours.

Surrounded by silence
and dry far away whispers.

Only like this, can I once again
see your ocean eyes
and hear your voice
so tender and slow.

Only like this, can I
once again feel
the warmth of your arms
wrapped around my waist.

Only like this, do I dare
to offer up my hand
into the profound darkness.

That is when the wind
and the ancestors
return you to me.

And for one divine moment,
I know that the dead
remain in life.

Stephanie Sorady

Grief's Hunger

Grief devours time
like I consume carbs
when trying not to feel.

In the blink of an eye,
massive chunks of life are gone.

Feed yourself with patience,
compassion and the bitter sweetness
of cherished memories.

Savor the tastes of healing
because despite what grief may have you
believe, there are no time limits here.

<u>When You are Grieving</u>

Cry as much you need to
or do not cry at all.

Remember it's okay to laugh again,
and share joyful stories of your lost love.

Go ahead and breathe
new life into your old memories
and add them into your todays
as often as you need.

Be as fucking angry as you want
that a piece of your heart
has temporarily left you.

You have lost something that was
as well as many things that could have been.
So, do not waste your time asking for permission
to grieve in whatever way you need.
Take all the time that there is.

Stephanie Sorady

Mr. Nice Guy

My wrists are bound
inside his fists;
my screams
fall flat on his
small sweaty ears.

Just one kiss
he insists,
as he presses
me against
the sharp edges
of a forced *yes*.

*We've been friends
for seven years.*

He deserved this,
he had earned this
always being
kinder than
the other guys.

*I've always been
a patient guy.*

*You let me drive
you home tonight.*

He recites
the evidence
of a contract
I never agreed to sign.

Just one kiss
he insists
as my screams
are muffled into cries
because he
is a nice guy.

What Do You Want From Me?

He asks with desperation bleeding from his eyes.
We're surrounded by the wreckage of another drunken fight,
and even though he's asked me the same exact question
about a thousand times, I can't give him an answer.

Truth is I know what I want, but I also know it's wrong.
I want him to worship me while giving me space.
I want him to save me, and let me play the hero.
I want him to lick all my wounds and tell me they taste sweet.

As the light of dawn drenches the room, I can see
scratch marks across his face, and a small miracle
begins to emerge from the cracks. A knowing grows
in my belly, and I can feel it fluttering around as his
question hangs in the air between us.
What do you want from me?

Nothing someone whispers.
It's not about you, this mature voice explains.
I want so much more, I need so much more
but it has to come from me.

That same day I washed my face and,
mustered the courage to get some help
with the hope that one day I could be my own
devout hero.

Stephanie Sorady

Anger

The white
hot
sword
that severed
my chains,
one
by
one.

The unlikely
protector
I so desperately
needed.

The first
harrowing step
I took
towards freedom.

Anger kept me sane.
Anger kept me safe.
Anger kept me away
from you.

Stephanie Sorady

My First Therapy Session

I don't know where to park.
There are no open meters on
the street and no "park here
if you're going crazy" lot.
Once I find a spot, a whole
new madness ensues.

Do I need to push a button
to let her know I'm here?
What happens if I push
the button too soon? Will
I look desperate? Or will
I look stupid if I don't
press it at all?

She is a small woman with
a big cackling laugh. I
silently hope that I can
laugh like that again someday.
Will this help me get there?
Normally, I would have
prayed, not hoped, but
I'm not sure God answers
my prayers these days.

There are books everywhere
and that makes my heart
feel a little bit more at home.
But what really does it for me
is the way she listens
when I speak. Her gaze is soft
and steady, not a hint of

judgement in the way she
nods along as my layers
slowly peel off.

Despite myself, I cry
from nervousness, grief,
anger, confusion and
all the other feelings
I cannot yet name.
My tears fill the room
and flood the office,
submerging this happy
woman's fancy therapist
things.

I profusely apologize
as shame attempts to
consume me. But she
won't allow it. She
tells me that shame
has no power here.

Fifty minutes later,
it's over. I walk out
not knowing if this
will work, or what
else I can expect.
But as I get back
in my car to drive
away, it crosses my mind
that.

maybe God was
listening to my prayers
afterall.

Stephanie Sorady

M is for Medicine

Movement is medicine
Music is medicine.
Mindfulness is medicine.
Minding your business is medicine.
Maintaining a boundary is medicine.
Anything that makes your soul go
mmm is medicine.

How Healing Began

The heavens didn't open.
It didn't look like a glitzy movie scene.
The angels didn't rejoice in song.
I heard no roaring of thunder,
and saw no parting of the seas.

But there was a need,
and a calling for more.

Like a seed that call grew
bigger, brighter, bolder.

Until it breached the surface,
and bloomed into something
I never knew was possible,
- hope.

Diagnoses

Clinical depression,
generalized anxiety disorder,
post traumatic stress,

It was my first visit to a psychiatrist,
and I was amazed at how cool and
confident she seemed laying out
these terms in front of me,
like a deck of playing cards.

Part of me felt seen,
as if the doctor had said
I believe you,
It's all right here,
I can see the battle scars,

while the other bits of me
felt small and condensed
into meaningless nonsense
and cold clinical codes.

I left her office carrying the weight
of each word in my shaking arms,
clinical depression,
generalized anxiety disorder,
post traumatic stress,

Who was I to claim such pain?
Was what I had been through
worthy of these labels?
Was this evidence that I was
weak or strong?

It took me time to understand
that a diagnosis is not
a definition of who you are
and all that you will be.

It took compassion for me
to comprehend that a diagnosis is
a tool meant to be used
by you,
for you,
so that you can do
all the marvelous things
you were meant to.

Stephanie Sorady

Perfectionist

I wonder where she keeps
all that pressure to perform
all things
perfectly
effortlessly
in order to ensure
everyone else is
appeased.

Does she hide it in her day planner?
Does she swallow it in the mornings
with her flat tummy pills?
Does she tuck it into her worn down running shoes?

Or is all that pressure
sitting at the tip of her nose
monitoring the way she breathes,
hiding in plain sight?

Can you see it?
Will you help her release it?

Stephanie Sorady

When You Feel Jealous

Take a moment to pause
let the slimy,
spiteful,
salty
feelings rise,
see the thing you covet
in your mind's eye.

Is it her high paying job?
His picture perfect family?
Her unbelievable body?
Or their confidence to be,
exactly who they want to be?

At this point you may
want to hide these feelings away,
and pretend like envy doesn't have
it's hot and sweaty hand
clasped around your heart.

Now is the time to turn the tables,
get curious and ask your envy,
What are you trying to tell me?

Maybe you don't desire
her position,
but you long to feel
valued and seen.

Maybe you don't ache for
a big family,
but you'd give anything
to find a loving community.

Maybe jealousy is telling you
it's time to show more love
to your own body.

When you feel jealous,
let the feelings rise,
get curious, stay open,
and you may be
surprised at the answers
you'll find.

Stephanie Sorady

Odio el Verano

Odio el verano
por las expectativas de
amor y aventura que,
por alguna razon,
el destino mantiene
siempre fuera de mi alcance.

Pero más que nada
odio el verano por su calor.
Pesado, húmedo e inevitable

Un calor que me saca
de mi mundo interior
y me devuelve al cuerpo
del que huí hace años,
para protegerme
de las críticas constantes.

Sea delgada,
pero no demasiado,
con curvas,
pero no parezcas vulgar,
debes ser deseable
pero nunca debes desear.

Kiss from God

¿Cómo podría quedarme
en un cuerpo que nunca fue
realmente mío?

Pero en el verano...
no tengo más remedio
que volver a este
cuerpo que segun
si es mío
e aún se siente
tan desconocido.

Para respirar
remojar
recargar
y recordar.

¿Qué pasaría si este verano
dejo ir el odio que ha
estado dentro de mí?

Y en cambio elijo
paciencia, compasión
y tal vez - algo de alegría,
para poder sentir solo un poco
del amor y la aventura
que el verano siempre proclama.

Stephanie Sorady

I Hate Summer

I hate summer,
the expectations of
love and adventure that
for some reason,
the fates always keep
just out of my reach.

But more than anything
I hate summer for its heat.
Heavy, wet, and unavoidable

A heat that takes me
out of my internal world
and brings me back to the body
I ran from years ago
to protect me
from the constant critiques.

> *Be slim,*
> *but not too much,*
> *with curves,*
> *not so vulgar,*
> *you must be desirable,*
> *but you should never desire.*

How could I stay
in a body that never
belonged to me?

But in the summer…

I have no choice
but to go back to this
body that allegedly
is mine yet feels
so unknown,

To breathe
soak in
recharge
and remember.

What if this summer
I let go of that hate?

And instead I choose
patience, compassion
and maybe - some joy,
to be able to taste
a bit of that love and adventure
that summer always promises.

Stephanie Sorady

Shiny Pieces

It took a long time to recognize,
that I am not a pile of junk,
just random fragments of shattered glass.

Now I see - I'm a collection,
of where I've been,
What I've lived through,
and all I will grow to be.

These bits and pieces make me,
A mosaic of hope.

Your Emotions Are Not the Enemy

Not the loud ones
not the stabbing ones
not the dragging ones
not the ones that make you sweat
not the ones that give you chills
not the ones that push
and not the ones that pull you back into yourself.

Your emotions are not the enemy,
no matter how messy or painful
they may be.

Emotions are your north star
in a human world that can
often appear so dark.

Be present with them
when they seek your attention;
shake them loose
from your body
when you've learned
all that you can.

Make peace with your emotions,
    so it becomes easier for you to be with others,
    so it becomes easier for you to be with yourself.

Stephanie Sorady

Kiss From God
Part 1

I was born with
purple watercolor marks
up and down my left arm.

Spiraling splotches
that sometimes remind me
of bougainvilleas in bloom.

My parents worried that
people would ask rude questions,
kids would be cruel,
and that I'd start
to conceal my arm in shame.

To help ease the discomfort of being different,
they quickly taught me the proper names,
birthmark in English y *lunar* en español.

But when folks inevitably asked,
What's that on your arm?
My young unsullied heart,
was quick to respond:
This is a Kiss From God!

Kiss From God
Part 2

The part of your body
you were told to abandon
and thus it makes you cringe
when you pass a mirror,
that is a Kiss From God.

The longing that wakes you
in the dark of night and whispers
you were meant for more
but others says it's just a fool's dream,
that is a Kiss From God.

The thing that you need to do
differently that everyone else around you
whether that be how you
move, speak, read, love or heal,
that is a Kiss From God.

If there are parts of you
that someone else
has foolishly deemed
dangerous
wrong
or strange,

do not be afraid
to proclaim,

This is a Kiss From God!

Stephanie Sorady

Love Yourself

Love yourself
without doubts
without shame
without explanations.

Love yourself
with desire
with pride
with each breath.

Love yourself
in times of sorrow
and times of joy,
in sacred places
and the most mundane spaces.

Today, tomorrow and always,
because you deserve it.

Ámate

Ámate
sin dudas
sin vergüenza
sin explicaciones

Ámate
con ganas
con orgullo
con cada respiro

Ámate
en tiempos de dolor,
y de alegría.
En lugares sagrados
y en los más mundanos.

Hoy, mañana y siempre,
porque tú lo mereces.

Finding Freedom

Depression feels like a cramped cage.
Anxiety reeks of purgatory,
and codependency is a pair
of invisible restraints.

Getting out feels far from easy,
but the only person in this world
strong enough to find their way
back to freedom
is you.

My dear, it has *always* been you.

Healing

Is not
a destination
we reach
where life becomes
a breezy island paradise.

Healing is
a winding road
made of
dark tunnels and
breathtaking views.

There are no road signs,
but plenty of pit-stops
to pause and rest a while.

Healing does not
mean your pain
stops.
It means that
pain is no longer
in the driver's seat.

Unseen Growth

You worry your life has withered,
like the dry and crinkled leaves of an autumn tree.
But have you seen what lies beneath?
There is more to growth than
blooming flowers and ripe fruit.
Do not overlook your tough and tangled roots,
reaching for the Earth's heart, unwilling to give up.
This season has been harsh and cold,
but do not disregard how deeply you've grown.

Full Heart

A heart that drinks
from a cup

filled to the brim
with gratitudes'
soothing spirits

does not crave
the intoxications
of external validation.

How I Used To Handle Problems

I'd feel the familiar itch of,
Maybe now it's time to quit?
But since making decisions
has never been my strong suit,
I'd head to the fridge instead.

Two bowls of cheerios,
a handful of tortillas chips,
three - okay five - chunks
of dark chocolate bliss,
all washed down by only
half a bottle of two buck chuck.

That's when my stomach would ache,
Maybe now it's time to take a break
and decide how you want to live?

But I'd skillfully pretend I couldn't hear a thing,
over the sounds of social media dances
and beautiful women I've never met
informing me that a capsule wardrobe
and glassy skin is all I'd need to finally
breathe a small sigh of relief.

When that wouldn't work
I'd lose myself in a boy instead,
convinced by fairytale myths
that a prince could one day
rescue me from this untouchable pain.

But the man was never as good
as the savior legend in my head,
so then it's back into bed
to cry and sleep then cry some more.

Until one day my therapist butts in,
That sounds like you're numbing.
Stunned and uncertain I reply,
Are you sure? I thought this was living.

¿Qué es la terapia?

La terapia no es un interrogatorio
o validación perversa
que no estás completo.
Lo más importante es que
nunca debería ser una violación de
tu derecho divino a la autodeterminación
y cómo eliges curarte.

La terapia debe ser tu reclamo,
un viaje
un recuerdo
un bálsamo
un espacio sagrado
donde puedes aceptar
al asombroso ser humano que eres.

What is therapy?

Therapy is not an interrogation
or perverse validation
that you are not whole.
Most importantly, it should
never be a violation of
your divine right to self-determination
and how you choose to heal.

Therapy should be your reclamation,
a voyage
a remembrance
a balm
a sacred space
where you get to be
simply who you are.

Full Heart

A heart that drinks
from a cup

filled to the brim
with gratitudes'
soothing spirits

does not crave
the intoxications
of external validation.

Wise Woman

I once knew a wise woman. She built her life on
art, love, and play. I gazed upon her life's work
and legacy shining bright around us like precious
jewels, and I could not help but covet such a treasure.
How did you do it? She smiled, lines spread across
her face mapping out the adventures she had lived.
With a gracious nod my wise woman replied,
'I wanted this life for such a long time.
One day I decided it was time to stop wanting.
Something had to change. I chose to love myself
enough to take it.'

Self Love Looks Like

Saying *I choose me*
Even when it means,
someone else may not like it.

Saying I *choose me*
No matter how hard
that decision may be.

Saying I choose me
In spite of being ambushed
with other people's needs.

Saying *I choose me*
Day after day,
because I am worth it.

At Last

Curled up on the couch,
       covered with the warmth
          of afternoon sun and abue's blue blanket

I am seized by the realization.
       That I am alone,
          but not lonely.

After years of dumping myself
       into the desires of someone else,
          followed by half-assed attempts.
             To find my way back,

I finally did it,
       I chose me.

I am alone,

       Alone - at last!

Stephanie Sorady

Why Did I Become a Therapist?

Once, I was almost crushed
beneath the painful weight
of never feeling seen.

But that pain did not stop me
from wanting to see others.

Wholly, plainly, honestly
without judgement and
brimming with unconditional
compassion.

In the therapy room,
time slows and expands
all at once (typical
of sacred spaces).

There is nowhere else
I want, or need, to be
then right there,
seeing you.

My clients have
saved my life
more times than even I
likely recognize.

The way these beautiful humans
get back up to fight, forgive and
find themselves
time and time again,
fills my soul like no
Earthly or otherworldly
moments ever could.

Why did I become a therapist?
Once, I did not feel heard
but that didn't stop me from
hearing the importance of
your words.

Permission Slip

You have permission to cry,
you have permission to fall,
you have permission to make
embarrassing mistakes,
you have permission to question
all of the "truths" you've been told,
you have permission to grow,
you have permission to take risks
and live a life even bigger than
your parent's noble dreams,
you have permission to rest a while
in the pursuit of what sets your soul on fire.
You have permission to be, or not be,
whatever you desire.

Crazy

You are not   crazy
for feeling things
so deeply.

The world is   crazy
demanding that you
numb.

<u>Mindfulness for Beginners</u>

When you feel the warmth of the sun

        rest upon your face,

stop a while,

        soften your gaze,

allow each and every cell

        to soak in the sacred rays.

Do not turn away

        and dive back into your next to-do;

let the universe's love

        nourish the deepest parts of you.

Two Chairs

We sit in silence. Inside the austere walls of a beige government building. He is slightly hunched in a small ugly chair. The kind of chair you typically see in frigid hospital waiting rooms. I sit in the bigger black computer chair. It's still cheap and ugly but it's the "expert" chair. The man across from me is old enough to be my father, so the chair doesn't fool anyone. I am not the expert here. I am the listener. The witness. The perspective giver. But not the expert. That's all him. He's about to show me something that he has deemed disgusting. I can tell because he prefaced this pregnant pause with, "I've never told anyone this before…not even my wife…" His wife is his best friend and I know he wishes he could show her whatever it is he's about to show me. But sometimes it's easier to share our secrets with the non-experts.

My mind flashes back to the first time I sat in the little chair across from my own therapist, reluctantly reaching down into the depths of myself to show her my own hideous truth. I liked her right away because she was half-Cuban, and I'm half-Mexican so I thought she might know what it feels like to never be enough of one thing. I hope that Mr. Q likes me too. He immigrated from Guatemala as a boy. We both enjoy familiar sounds of Spanglish in our sessions. These seemingly small things can make the space between our chairs feel less expansive. He gulps loudly, pulling me back into my seat. His wide brown eyes meet mine, and his right hand twitches to absently touch his watch. He shows me the burden he's been hiding for so long and I'm not surprised by what I see. It's the same thing I showed my therapist.   It's his humanity.

Stephanie Sorady

Acceptance

My mind buzzes and hums
with the familiar rhythms
of indecision, uncertainty,
and desires that were buried
long ago.

The bees float back and forth
from perfect flower to perfect flower,
and I cannot contain my envy

Thus, I crouch into the Earth
and spill my secrets to the bees:
I wish I was like you
and always knew what to do,
selfless, pious and effortlessly
prioritizing everyone but you.

But you are not a bee they say,
and just like that the buzzing stops.
I brush the dirt off my knees
and rise with newfound ease
because I am not a bee.

Grounded

Everytime the universe God, ancestors, gravity,
has brought you to your knees, maybe it's been
because you need to come a little closer
to the Earth beneath holding up those hurried feet.

Stephanie Sorady

Break-Through

That moment in therapy
when a life giving breath is taken,
and you hear something, somewhere
shatter.

Like a porcelain figurine that has been
covered in dust and resting (a little too comfortably)
on the same shelf for so long, then suddenly
gets knocked straight into the ground.

But when you look down, you are greeted
with relief. Nothing is broken here;
it's the chance to rebuild something new.

You are not broken;
you are breaking-through

You Are Not Crazy

She takes apart her heart
slowly at first but eventually,
a bit more rough
with a healthy dose of rage.

Once she's done,
she lays the revered organ
neatly on the table
(because even now she
craves control).

Next, she unveils a small note
that must've been
tucked away
in her heart
for very long.

Without a word
she hands me the
crumpled little page,
gently I unwrinkle it
and find a single request written:
Please, tell me I'm not crazy.

Trauma

Re-arranges the brain
and unfortunately, this change
isn't neatly contained;
it moves through our bodies,
emotions manifesting as physical pain,

migraines
back aches
sleepless nights
all your energy - drained.

Maybe you lash out at your loved ones,
losing your patience more and more.
Maybe it feels better to stay inside,
away from the grinding irritation
of crowds, loud noises, and blinding lights.
Maybe it's that certain smell,
that comes out of nowhere
dragging you back to hell.

You've done nothing wrong;
somewhere on this path
all of your alarm systems
were switched to ON.

Kiss from God

After trauma, nothing is the same.
With the intent to protect
mind and spirit,
the body will keep fighting
against dangers that
exist in the past.

Will it ever be okay
to put the armor away,
to let go of control,
to be willing to make mistakes?

Yes,

new neurons
new nervous system
new opportunities for growth,

if we can sit through the fire
if we can learn how to cool the flames,
if we can summon the strength to
shift through ashes day after day.

There is more to uncover,
more compassion
more connection
more meaning

Trauma comes for us all
but so does transformation.

Stephanie Sorady

Abundance

Is not a six-figure salary,
endless vacations,
or even millions of followers
with your name pressed into
their eager thumbs.

Abundance is the ability to find joy,
in subtle ways, soft and refreshing
like the sounds and smells of summer rain.

Abundance lies in the decision to make peace
with the darkest corners of your mind,
so that you can finally
pull back the dusty curtain
and let the morning's light shine.

Abundance is not obtained
through external transactions,
It's unwrapped from the inside,
a gift from God you don't need to earn.

Reminder for the Bad Days

When you woke up late,
only ate junk food,
said something awkward at work,
forgot about your doctor's appointment
and got charged a $20 no show fee,
sat in traffic for an hour,
didn't have time to shower,
got left on read by the crush you DM'd,

My friend, do not forget, you deserve
to feel love
on the bad days too.

<u>For Therapists</u>

You cannot fix your clients,
because people are not broken.

Systems are broken,
all the Goddamn time.

But not people,
we adapt, evolve, survive.

<u>Love: Before
and After Healing</u>

Love used to look like
one foot in the door
and the other out.

Love used to sound like
jealous accusations
and long nights
of fighting for attention.

Love used to feel like
sand slipping through
my frenzied hands.

Love used to smell like
something sickenly sweet
that you can't escape.

Love used to live outside,
in a far away place.

But now,

Love looks like
an outstretched hand,

Love sounds like
the steady rush of waves,

Love feels like
solid ground beneath my feet,

Love smells like
a warm cozy home,
hope, and possibility.

Love lives in me.

Stephanie Sorady

Su Primer Amor

Wrote poems about her,
just like I do.
Because my abuela
is the type of woman,
you hope to immortalize.

How To Love You

My abuela loved my abuelo
the way una reina loves to reign,

My mother loves my father
the way a cactus soaks in sun,

I don't always know
how to love you,
Maybe, I'm not built the same?

I'm not the woman who will
rule your heart,
or bask in your warmth.

I may not always know to love you,
but I promise you,
I do.

If Your Heart Were a Book

If your heart were a book,
I'd ache to touch every single page.
But not to simply flip through
with casual irreverence,
like some checkout counter magazine.

I'd take my time to delight in each word,
commune with every chapter
and inhale the smell of
your paper and ink.

I'd carry your book in my purse,
place it beneath my pillow,
memorize the most clever lines,
and recite them in the shower.

If your heart were a book,
I'd make your story my holy text.

What Lives On

Love changes
everything it touches,

altering chemistry,
reprogramming minds,

moving mountains,
and leaving marks
we can't always see.

Even when these
fragile frames
are long gone,
love lives on.

<u>Si Te Preguntas ¿Esto es amor?</u>

El amor no manipula,
el no amor no golpea,
el amor no hace promesas
que nunca pretende cumplir,
el amor no culpa
en lugar de pedir disculpas,
el amor no limita el alcance de tus alas

No,

El amor te eleva y te anima a brillar,
el amor te ve exactamente como eres,
con todos tus defectos y virtudes,
y se queda deslumbrado por cada parte de ti.
El amor te mira y se pregunta,
¿cómo puedo dar lo mejor de mí?

If You're Asking Yourself: Is this Love?

Love doesn't manipulate,
love doesn't strike,
love doesn't make promises
it never means to keep,
love does not pass the blame
in place of asking for forgiveness.
Love does not limit the reach of your wings,

No,

Love lifts you up and inspires you to shine,
love sees you exactly as you are,
with all of your flaws and strengths
and is in awe of what it sees.
Love looks at you and asks,
How can I give them the best of me?

Like a Lady

Sit like a lady
I am told for the
millionth time.

So,

I spread my legs
far and wide,
opening my
strong goddess thighs,
across valleys,
through forests,
over the humps
of mountains.

I stuff my face
with lust,
say dirty words
like *no,*
demand pockets
then fill those
pockets with confidence
and refuse to feel shame
about the bulging
of my breasts,
or the ripples
on my thighs.

I sit tall, wide and proud,
ready to birth
a more just world

like a badass lady would.

Married Woman

I want to reach across the table,
knock the phone out of your hand,
and erase the years that have passed
between us so that you'll grab me
by the waist and kiss me
like you used to
when there was no church or state
binding us to sit here day after day
while the urge to rip
each other's clothes off slowly
evaporates into thin air.
I want to smack the sleepiness out of our lives
and ask if you ever think about
the days when we made love in cars,
I want you to notice the rumbling
beneath my skin and unravel me
to let it out, even if that means you
might get burned. I want you to forget
that I'm your wife, so that I can be a woman again.

<u>Prayer & Sisterhood</u>

Will you pray for me tonight?
Because right now my soul is dry
and yearns to soak in the sacred
sweetness of sisterhood.

But don't bother praying with
the men who shut our ancient
mothers out of the spiritual
realms they created.

Yes - the same men who made
church a judgemental place,
instead of a community known by
the songs of its people.

In your invocations I ask
that you do not enlist the help
of the false prophets
who claim women are
either revered virgins
or nothing at all.

These are the holier-than-thou men
who want us to forget,
that Magdalen was the Savior's
confidant and truest friend.

Sister - your prayers have revived my
divine body and limitless soul.

Now together let us cleanse the Earth
from the sins of heretics who were
so threatened by the power
of a woman's pleasure,
that they created entire cults
to convince us
that a life of pain was the only way

Ode to My Ancestors

I am the descendent of licentious pagans
who dared to love the land they lived on,
hunting with reverence and communing
with the gods and goddesses like wild
heathens do.

I am the descendent of rough and uncivilized
women who bore their naked bodies beneath the moon
and breastfed babies as their skin soaked in the sun,
some with braided ribbons in their long black hair,
some with blue war paint on their torsos marking them
as stars.

I am the descendent of blood soaked warriors
whose screams and roars echo in my throat;
a community that refused to relinquish
their way of living and their homes
without a fight.

I am the descendent of my heroes,
I am the heir of their freedom.

Grandpa Ernie's Advice on Golf
(and life)

When you're starting out,
find one good teacher
and trust
what they have to say.

Actually do what they tell you to!
Put it all into practice
and see what does
and does not
work for you.

Once they've taught you what they know,
don't look for more teachers,
ask others for advice,
or look around to see how
someone else is playing.

Just focus on your game

because before you know it,
you'll be filled with so much
competing information
you won't even be able to swing your club anymore,
let alone actually hit the ball.

Pick a good teacher,
keep showing up to play,
and trust your body will know the rest.

Stephanie Sorady

Children of Immigrants

You are warriors,
and you do not need
to be invincible.

You are adaptable,
and you do not need
to bend so that others
feel comfortable.

You are familiar with
the many faces of sacrifice,
and you can befriend
abundance too.

You are the bridges between worlds
connecting cultures with every step,
and no one else can define
who you are.

You are the inheritor of ancestral dreams,
and you are destined to go after
dreams that are uniquely your own.

Children of immigrants,
you are strong,
you are worthy,
you can have it all.

A Bridge

It is my
burden
blessing
birthright

To savor the stories
of my cultures
separated by
land, oceans and
man-made lines in the sand.
United in their
faith, strength, and humility

I do not belong here
nor there,
But perhaps I can be
the bridge between worlds.

After all,
only something so unique
could achieve such a feat.

Stephanie Sorady

Losses of Translation

If only I could explain to my head
los huecos que existen en mi corazón al no poder
expresarme completamente en inglés ni español.
Two unequal halves of me exist,
as I stumble through an either/or world.
My cultures are often lost in translation,
mi identidad no tiene patria.
So I roam wondering
if I'll ever really be home.

Ojalá

A Spanish word,
whose closest relative in English
is *hopefully,*
but that word falls flat
and tastes empty in comparison.

Ojalá has proud Arabic roots,
stemming from the phrase
wa sha allah
should God will it.

We say it as an invocation,
to summon holy spirits
upon particularly uncertain times,
where the answers lie beyond
the reach of frail human hands.

There will be jobs and opportunities in the United States,
Ojalá,
Our familia will be reunited again someday,
Ojalá,
Every sacrifice we make for our children will be worth it,
Ojalá,

Hopefully just doesn't cut it.
This utterance is a prayer,
a demonstration of
faith, perseverance and surrender.

Stephanie Sorady

Guardian Abuelo

After a day marked and muddled
by endless medical exams,
a doctor enters the room and
proclaims: appendicitis!
Like I've won a carnival prize.

Funny enough, I find comfort
in the diagnosis and my mind flickers
to you. The abuelo I never knew.
I've been told I have your mouth,
with a thicker bottom lip and
compact, but prominent, pout.

I also heard you were an artist,
like me? Except you played
La bateria and I write poetry.

You died of an appendicitis
at the age of fifty-nine,
and this diagnosis is another
genetic breadcrumb
for me to savor. A small
mark linking me to
the abuelo I never knew.

It was you that I prayed to
as they wheeled me into
the crisp white operating room.

Mi angelito de la guarda,
My guardian angel.
While the drugs lulled me into sleep,
I heard the beat of your drums,
a slow and steady ancestral buzz,
soothing me, you are not alone.

To this day, I can still hear
their enveloping beats
eager to comfort me,
when I am alone or in pain.

Stephanie Sorady

What About Mi Gente?

It would be easier for other people
if I wasn't Mexican.
That is, if I stopped claiming
my mother's homeland,
my heritage.

Being part Mexican with such
pale skin can be a haunting
sight for some.
Inevitably there's a voice
that feels the need
to question me:

But aren't you white?
How does that work?
Can you prove it?
Alright then, say something
in Spanish!

Confusion turns into discomfort
and if I refuse to play
the 'convince me' game,
discomfort creeps into rage.

Admittedly, I am not what you imagine
when you think of a Mexican-American
or Latina woman - but here I stand.

My phenotypes favored my father
Irish-blooded Brooklyn boy,
and while my heart holds
a tender place for Éire and

my foremothers that crossed
an ocean so that their babies
could eat,
I had no say in how I look.
I didn't do a thing to earn
the protective cloak or umerited praise
this white skin provides
in both my cultures.

It would be less confusing for other people,
if I wasn't Mexican.

But what about my mamá?
What about the tías, primas and abuelita
who helped raise me?
What about my love for Joan Sebastian?
Mas alla del sol!

What about my constant cravings for
pozole rojo (despite being a vegetarian)?
What about the sleepless nights I've spent
huddled with my primos because
we feared la llorona coming to take us away?

What about all the rezos I dutifully
memorized so Diosito would keep
my family safe?
Santo ángel de mi guarda,
What about my indigenous ancestors
who I refuse to erase?
Mi dulce compañia,
What about mi gente?
no me desampares ni de noche ni de día,
What about me?

Stephanie Sorady

Half

Being "half" of something means that if you're not always
digging up your roots and showing them off as proof
people won't believe that you are whole

Whole

But whether or not they see the culture intertwined
in the grip of your roots, you are a living, breathing,
heart beating, reminder to the whole world just how
connected we are. Countless moments and movements
and have waited for someone like you to stick your
hands into the Earth then raise them to the heavens
and proclaim,

Yes, I belong here too!

Stephanie Sorady

What's Wrong With Easy?

Life is already jagged and harsh.
What's so wrong with wanting
your skin to be drenched
in silks so smooth it's like
rippled water you can touch?

Who said you need to carry
a cross in order to reach
promised land?
Maybe if you need to
fight, chase, coerce
and force it into your life
it may not have been meant   for you.

Slowly loosen your grip,
learn to let go,
allow your life to feel easy.
Let yourself believe
you can lay claim
to that ease.

From Your Big Sister

One day, you'll be old enough for me to show you
the scars on the bottoms of my feet, the bruises
on my back from walking as far as I could
carrying all the weight that my body could handle
with the hope that one day, the two of you might
roam this world a little more protected and prepared.

One day, you'll be old enough to show me all
the things I missed while you were bearing your
own burdens and discovering brand new dreams.
The days will stretch out before us giving us plenty
of time to catch up on things, and the Earth
will welcome our exchange of stories the way it
welcomes fresh rain after years of drought.

One day, we will all be grown enough to
kneel side by side and repair the foundations
of our ancestral home. One brick at a time.
Not out of obligation, or riddled with resentments
but nourished by joy and the knowledge that
even though each of us took different paths,
we all wound up here, together and whole.

Stephanie Sorady

My Breath

My breath flows
in and out of me
like God's love
with humility,
power, and ease.

    My breath lets go
    of what no longer
    serves or uplifts
    me. I breathe
    in a gentler future
    and exhale the
    limitations
    of yesterday.

My breath has always
been with me and
will keep on
supporting me until
my soul is ready
to return home.

My breath is my
secret weapon,
my constant
companion ready to
ease me back
into the present
when my mind has gone.

My breath is
medicine, calming
psyche, spirit
and soul.
When I feel
angry, rushed or
overwhelmed
my breath is there
to comfort me.
In through the nose
and out through the mouth.
One…two…three…
one…two…three…

Kiss from God

I Come Awake at Night

I come awake at night,
when the sun has laid its head to rest
and mothers have carried their children to bed.
When the stars have declared its time for dancing
and no one is around to ask me for - anything.

I come awake at night,
because as a little girl this was no time for sleeping.
Our home was loud, but my loneliness was louder.
How could I close my eyes when the adults
were doing so much living?

I come awake at night,
as stealthy animals rise from the dusk
eager to commence the hunt.
When my mind feels fierce and
my pen stays steady.

Thank you God for the sunlight,
that feeds our skin and soil,
but I will take the darker times
because I've grown strong
in the sweet solemnity of night.

Stephanie Sorady

For my Future Children

I didn't grow up with a backyard.
If it had been otherwise,
I would write you a poem about how
that backyard had a garden and
that garden had some weeds.
I'd tell you all about how
I had to get my hands dirty,
freckling beneath the sun,
to dig up each and every one.

Then I'd (hopefully) create
an illuminating metaphor
about the shady trees
and optimistic sunflowers
I planted in lieu of those weeds.

Mis amores, I would've guaranteed you many things.
But I didn't grow up with a backyard - there was no garden.

If there's one thing I've learned so far
on this journey from hurting to helping,
it's the importance of humility.
Right now, I don't even know whose womb
you'll grow from. That's more than okay,
That's how it's meant to be.
But there are a few things I do know,
a handful of humble promises I can make:

You'll always be safe in my arms.
You'll make mistakes and feel pain.
I will probably make more mistakes.
Siempre te haré té de manzanilla
when your tummies or hearts ache.
Your voices carry weight in our home.
I love you not in spite of who you are,
but because of it.
We may or may not have a yard,
but we will have a garden,
and together we will plant whatever we want.

Stephanie Sorady

Animals Adapt

I'm amazed by how the animals have adapted
to living in and around our messes.
From the squirrels that scale telephone poles
or risk certain death when they sprint across a busy street,
To the bee hives that now occupy
buildings we placed in nature's way,
then left behind,
I cannot help but gawk
at the birds who refuse to lose
their cheerful morning songs
despite the fact that we've filled
the air, and their small lungs, with smog.
While we build, scroll and take control,
they adapt to our human chaos
with a sense of purpose and ease
that humans have been chasing all along.

By Candlelight

I pray,
I write,
I make love,
I bathe,
I dream,
by candlelight.

Because even though
I'd like to believe
creativity
flows through me
like rushing streams
of cool blue waters
in reality,
it eats through my flesh
like hungry flames.

I kiss,
I let go,
I admire my body,
I am gentle with myself,
I am present with others,
by candlelight.
While there is
beauty in the starkness
of light,
shadows soften the scars
and contour our strongest parts.

Stephanie Sorady

Here

Here,
in the cool room
of the new apartment
I can finally afford
as I hang white linen drapes.

Here,
while my love wraps
gentle hands around me
before he goes outside
to fill the hummingbird feeder
with sugar water.

Here,
in the natural rhythm of my breath,
deep and smooth, as my departed
loved ones smile upon me from above.

Here,
I am safe.

Kiss from God

Moment of True Love

In an unguarded moment
    I relished in her touch
warm, soft, strong
    Admiring the thickness of her thighs
ready to walk the whole Earth at any moment
    yet constantly rooted in the ground that bore her.
I gazed into her mossy green eyes
    small cracks forming around the corners
like roadmaps of all the times she smiled
or squinted her gaze in the bright sun.
For that brief and ecstatic moment
    I let myself be awed by how good it feels
to love myself.

Stephanie Sorady

Mental Health & Wellness Resources

If this book inspires you to explore additional mental health and wellness resources, please feel free to review and reference the resources listed below:

SAMHSA: Substance abuse and mental health services administration. Resources for substance use, mental health, and suicide prevention (también contiene recursos en español.) www.samhsa.gov

National Suicide Prevention Lifeline:
1-800-273-TALK (8255)

Crisis Text Line: For 24/7 crisis support text HOME to 741741

Self-Compassion: To learn practical steps to practice more compassion towards yourself take a look at the work of Dr. Kristin Neff at www.self-compassion.org

Meditation & Mindfulness: www.headspace.com

Therapist Directories:
Latinx Therapy - www.latinxtherapy.com
Inclusive Therapists - www.inclusivetherapists.com
Therapy for Black Girls - www.therapyforblackgirls.com
Therapy for Black Men - www.therapyforblackmen.org
Asian Mental Health Collective - www.asianmhc.org
Institute for Muslim Mental Health - www.muslimmentalhealth.com

Or call the number on the back of your insurance card for a list of providers.

Disclaimer: This book is for entertainment purposes. In no way does any content in this book substitute clinical mental health services. If you are in need of clinical services, reach out to a licensed health professional for more information. If you or someone else is experiencing a crisis, please call 911, a crisis line, or go to your nearest emergency room.

Acknowledgements

I must start off by thanking my wonderful husband, Andrew Iverson, who has been reading first drafts, quelling fits of self-doubt and cheering me on since day one. I couldn't ask for a better life partner. Thank you for never letting me quit and for never being annoyed all the times I said,"Sorry I wasn't listening - I was thinking about my book." You are my best friend, always.

To my parents, Ada Luz and T.J. Sorady, for consistently believing I was a "real writer" long before I ever did. You fill my life with wonderful stories, laughter and incredible food - thank you! To my siblings, Thomas and Sophia, who make me want to be the best version of myself. I cannot express what an honor it is to be your sister.

To my therapist, Bianca, for giving me the sacred space to cry, laugh and grow. So much of this book was made possible by the work we've done together, and I am eternally grateful.

A very special thanks goes to Davina Ferreira for teaching me, inspiring me and creating such a beautiful community of Latinx writers. This book, and many others, wouldn't be possible without you. To my Alegría writing familia who gave me the feedback and courage necessary to share my work. You are some of the most talented people I've ever known, and creating our work together is something I will always cherish. Thank you to the incredible artist and entrepreneur, Norma Rapko, whose art inspired the cover of this book. To see more of Norma's art please visit normarapko.com

To my high school English teacher, Karen McNally, who exposed me to life changing books and new ways of seeing the world. Every student deserves at least one Ms. McNally.

Last but certainly not least to the women in my family who came before, and whom I hope to honor with my work: Rosemary Sorady Simpson, Donna Anne Fisher, Grace Simpson, Antoinette Knight (Nana Banana), Maria Dolores Chavez Salgado, Evelia Arias Chavez, Olga Arias Chavez, Leticia Arias Chavez, Margarita Arias Chavez, Mirna Arias Chavez and many more beautiful souls.

About the Author

Stephanie Sorady is a poet, writer, and mental health professional born and raised in Los Angeles. As a result of her own experiences with anxiety, depression and post-traumatic stress, she is passionate about de-stigmatizing mental health topics and empowering readers through her work. Her writing also proudly incorporates her Mexican & Irish American background and explores themes such as mindfulness, grief/loss, self-love, feminism and spirituality. Stephanie received her Bachelor's in Social Sciences with an emphasis in Psychology from the University of Southern California and her Master's in Social Work from Columbia University. Stephanie loves making people laugh, traveling to hear the stories of others, re-watching her favorite T.V. shows, and learning to set boundaries like a badass. She lives with her husband, Andrew, her dog, Stella, and parakeet, Delta. *Kiss From God* is her first poetry collection.

Connect with the author:

Website: StephanieSorady.com
Instagram: @StephanieSorady_msw

www.ingramcontent.com/pod-product-compliance
Lightning Source LLC
Chambersburg PA
CBHW040423100526
44589CB00022B/2815